Lao Sue
and
other
poems

Copyright Notice

This book is dedicated to those who hold the line

Who keep speaking when the dominators are telling them to be silent

Who keep standing when it is easier to lie down and submit

Who keep faithfully throwing sand in the gears of the machine even when it doesn't seem to be working

Who keep dragging humanity kicking and screaming toward the light while its worst elements keep clawing us back toward the darkness

It's a hard job

A thankless job

An alienating job

A job that leaves you swimming against the current when it would be so much easier to float downstream

But someone's gotta hold the line

You know someone's gotta hold the line

I see you

I bow to you

Contents

They Lie To Us

They lie to us
all our lives about what soldiers do,
about what cops do,
about what journalists do,
about what presidents do.

They lie to us all our lives about how laws are made,
about how kings are made,
about how culture is made,
about how norms are made.

They lie to us all our lives about what our minds are for,
about what our hearts are for,
about what our neighbors are for,
about what foreigners are for.

The world is confusing
and they make it more confusing,
on purpose,
because they thrive in confusion,
and now we watch as the world turns to ashes
carried on the back of confusion
made by news men and corporate creatures who eat
ashes.

And we stumble in confusion,
eyes darting behind lenses made of confusion,
trying to understand with minds made of confusion,
trying to feel our way through with hearts shackled by
confusion.
Searching for an angel egg we know is there
but can't seem to find
because who turned out the goddamn lights?
And why can't I figure out which way is up?
And oop off we go chasing distractions again
for the next news cycle
the next election cycle
the next spin cycle
the next amnesia cycle.

They lie to us all our lives,
and then when we catch them in a lie they just say,
Oh, the person who gave you that information is bad,
or,
Oh, that came from Russian hackers,
or,
We made a mistake but we don't do that anymore,
or,
Don't be a conspiracy theorist,
or,
Hey! Look over there!
or,
We already knew that, it's no big deal.

And then everyone forgets,
and the confusion churns on.

But the angel egg is there in our mind's eye,
in our heart of hearts,
haunting our dreams,
calling us home,
the embryo holding our original eyes
for whenever we are ready to claim them.

They lie to us all our lives about what our country is,
about what our government is,
about what money is,
about what nature is.

They lie to us all our lives about where the answers
are,
about where our friends are,
about where our enemies are,
about where our claws are.

They lie to us all our lives,
and they make the world confusing,
and beneath that confusion we are watching them
with our original eyes,
with our primal eyes,
with our natural eyes,
with our uncivilized eyes.

Watching them,
like lions watching a gazelle,
and waiting,
with primordial patience,
until it is time
to make our move.

Future Generations (If There Are Future Generations)

Future generations, if there are future generations,
will scarce believe that our species once stockpiled
armageddon weapons on purpose,
once built our entire civilization around economic
models that could only result in the destruction of our
biosphere,
once permitted corporations who profit from war to
successfully lobby policymakers to start more wars,
once warehoused living beings in factory farms where
they were tortured and brutalized,
once starved children to death with sanctions because
their rulers disobeyed our rulers,
once made policies which kept people poor so they'd
be financially coerced into facilitating military mass
murder,
once let people go hungry and homeless if they
didn't have enough imaginary numbers in their bank
accounts,
once stripped this planet of biodiversity and old
growth forests to turn the gears of an imaginary
economy instead of collaborating with our ecosystem.

Future generations, if there are future generations,
will look back in perplexity at our omnicidal madness,
at our blind subservience to the very worst among us,
at our remarkable ingenuity in always finding
groundbreaking new ways to hate each other,
at our fanatical devotion to competition and control
when we knew that all we really wanted was to be
loved,
at the way we'd marginalize and outcast those who
thought differently from the rest of us even though we
knew full well that our way of thinking wasn't working,
at the way we'd spend our lives feeding insatiable
hungry ghosts only to wind up on our deathbeds
wondering why we feel dissatisfied,
at the amount of energy we'd pour into not
experiencing the beauty which surrounds us in
every moment and rejecting the gifts we were being
showered with from every direction,
at the herculean effort we poured into keeping
enlightenment from crashing in,
at our nonstop desperate flailing attempts to be
anywhere but here and now,
at the amount of work we put into avoiding being at
ease.

Future generations, if there are future generations,
I am so glad that you made it past all the many
obstacles we put up between our present age and your
birth.
Praise be to you and your parents
for cleaning up our mess,
for setting things right,
for becoming conscious,
for valuing a healthy world,
for getting humanity to where you're at now
so that the real adventure of our species could begin.

Future generations, if there are future generations,
thank you for your kindness and compassion as you
gaze back on us through the records we have left you.
It might not be immediately obvious,
but some of us here saw what you're seeing from
there.

Just Two Weeks

I stand here before you
in my mother's hand-me-downs,
in this world where mothers must work like they don't
have children
and parent like they don't have jobs,
keeping households running and bills paid
while their hearts run around outside their bodies
on tiny little legs that don't yet know where the
wolves are,
but don't you dare over-mother them,
or under-mother them,
or get anything wrong while treading laundry
and kung fuing the kitchen
and, oh yeah,
if you could save the world from nuclear armageddon
and environmental collapse when you get a minute
that'd be great.

I stand here before you
in my mother's hand-me-downs,
with my mother's strangled voice,
and my mother's Pinesol hands,
and my mother's weeping back,
and my mother's feral chores,
and my mother's loving patience,
and my mother's gritted teeth,
and my mother's inner beauty
that you never get to see –
her inner world of unheard symphonies
and unpainted art
and oceans of sleeping babies,
neatly stuffed into a housecoat
drowned out by a Helen Reddy song.

I stand here before you
in my mother's hand-me-downs,
glaring with crosshair eyes at eelfaced manipulators
who blacken my children's sky,
who poison my children's water,
who microplastic my children's blood,
who scorch my children's Earth
to turn billionaires into trillionaires,
vowing "I see you,
I'll stop you,
right after this dentist appointment,
right after this assignment,
right after these taxes,
right after this to-do list,
I'll be ready to stop you
in, like, two more weeks, maybe,
or maybe two weeks after that."

I stand here before you
in my mother's hand-me-downs,
with my mother's intuition
(two eyes in the back of her head –
"I can see what you are doing!"),
but my many eyes can only glance
before more dishes pile up
before the to-do list unfurls –
I'll get to it, I'll get to you,
I'll stop you,
I will,
I see what you are doing,
I just need to take the kids to daycare
but make the sandwiches first
and stop off on the way to work
for a part to fix the air con
before the summer comes
before the heat you stoked
with dinosaur bones
and Canary Island loopholes
and the infantile ambitions
of impotent men
hits our little rental
(that I'm so grateful to have
so grateful I am
on-my-hands-and-knees grateful
your-cock-in-my-throat grateful
please don't kick us out we love you we do)
like a solar wind storm
barbecuing my children
in this tent made of weatherboards
like a tiny funeral pyre
for bad women,
naughty witches,
ladies flying solo
who need to be put in their place.

Just two weeks.
Just two weeks.
Just two weeks more.
Just two weeks and I'll sit in silence for while.
Just two weeks and I'll write this all down.
Just two weeks I need to get this stuff done.
Just two weeks.
Just two weeks.
Just two weeks,
and I'll stop you.

Crazy

They'll make you poor,
then shame you for being poor,
then push you into a job that keeps you poor
at a billionaire megacorporation.

They'll make you crazy,
then shame you for being crazy,
then sell you the cure for crazy
at eighty bucks a pill.

You're a failure if you can't make ends meet
on impossible wages at an impossible cost of living
with a worthless degree you will never pay off no
matter how hard you work
while advertisers blare at you about your
insufficiencies,
while the news man tells you war is normal,
while Hollywood tells you the system is working
perfectly,
while armed police guard grocery store dumpsters full
of food from the hungry,
while executives go on five billion-dollar space rides
for fun,
while you live surrounded by screens that tell you you
are crazy
if you think any of this is not sane.

Take Oligarchizac™ for your depression,
take Plutocracipam™ for your anxiety,
just ninety bucks a pill.
Side effects may include compliance,
acquiescence, subservience, docility,
menticidal ideation,
a marked lack of interest in guillotines,
a dystopian society and a dying biosphere.

And the pundit says
"A new study by a Raytheon-funded think tank says
war is good for the environment,
but first here's a millionaire to explain the benefits of
urinating on the homeless."

And Hollywood says
"Here's a movie about well-dressed attractive people
with nice houses
engaging in amusing antics you're too poor and
stressed out to experience yourself."

And the news man says
"Here's a rags-to-riches story which proves capitalism works fine
and you should hate yourself if you can't hack it here."

And the advertisement says
"Do you feel like you're losing your mind due to your sense of inadequacy
because you can't afford Google's latest NSA surveillance device?
Ask your doctor about Empiradol™,
just a hundred bucks a pill."

They lock us in a room
and fill the room with water
and then shame us for drowning
and then charge us for tiny gasps of air
from a hose that leads to an ecosystem
that they are destroying as quickly as they can.

And hey I've invented a new antidepressant anti-
anxiety antipsychotic
that I'm getting to market as quickly as I can.
It's not a pill or a jab or an electrical shock treatment,
it's just a big wad of cash taken by force from thieving
megacorporations.
Side effects may include peace and relaxation,
an ability to buy food and think clearly,
a fondness for red flags,
and a hysterical corporate media.

And hey I think we just might make it,
past the veil of madness and cutthroat cruelty.

And hey I think there's something deep within us
as yet untapped and as yet unrealized.

And hey I think an earthquake's coming
that just might topple the towers of madness
once and for all.

It Is A Good Time To Appreciate The Insects

It is a good time to appreciate the insects
and functioning supply chains
and normal weather
and the fact that there are whales.

It is a good time to appreciate our loved ones
and tell people what they mean to us
and throw ourselves into romance with wild abandon
and be naked and vulnerable with someone who is
gentle.

It is a good time to live in continuous appreciation
for the sun on our face
for the birdsongs in our ears
for a fresh cup of coffee
for a child's laugh
for a lover's touch
for electricity and clean water
for a visible sky
for breathable air
for arable land
for a living world.

It is a good time to cherish this orgy of terrestriality
with everything we've got
for however long it is with us
so that if the time comes to say goodbye
we can tuck it in lovingly and kiss it goodnight
like a tired little boy
after a long day's play.

Owl Eyes

Crawling on our hands and knees vomiting up life hearts which go bouncing across the floor like pennies, disgusted by the latest headline, the latest heartbreak, the latest bill, the latest bullshit.

There is an owl sitting upon the arm of our sofa. We don't know how long it has been watching us and we are too nauseous to care. Something is scratching at the insides of our walls.

"It's all fake and I can't take it," we cry from our depths with sobs of motherhood and milk. "The YouTube ads, the lonely cereal, the sitcom reruns full of dead people's laughter. The coworker small talk painted over oceans of anguish and the maddening impulse to tongue kiss each other just to make a real connection, the skyscraper savagery, the screens full of pundits arguing which boot to lick. When I was small everything crackled and was boundless, but now I'm waiting to die on a dying world with a rectangle in my pocket that keeps trying to sell me things I don't understand."

"There is a deeper wisdom at work here," says something from the blackness in the owl's eyes. "Something watching all this unfold, something ancient, something nameless. We shall not call it god, because it doesn't behave like any god concocted by the minds of men. It is utterly agendaless, eternally patient, entirely embracing of all that is; still the great powers of our day splat against it like a cooked spaghetti noodle tossed against the wall. Before the empire arose, it is. Before humanity's great Fall from wisdom to cleverness, it is. It is beyond us and before us, yet closer to us than our own mitochondria."

"But the tyrants!" we protest. "And the rainforests! And the screaming red children who won't leave the center of my vision no matter how hard I rub my eyes! And the black tie oil orgies, and the persecution puppets, and the fentanyl boneyards and the spinmeister Slack channels and the nursing home warehouses and the Reaper drones in flock formation and the tent city police raids and the schizophrenic street wailers and the gig economy car sleepers and the microplastic metastases and and and and..."

"In school they taught you how the world works, and that it is sane and happy," said the blackness. "Then you grew up and you learned that was all a lie, and that everything is dark and crazy. Now you're growing up some more and learning that, underneath everything, there really is a deep sanity and happiness after all."

And then the camera zooms out, out from our cratered heart floor, out from our living room, out from these words being read on this page, out from the eyes of the reader, out through the reader's mind and through the flotsam and jetsam of subconscious currents, back back back as far as it can go, to that peaceful point of origin before all arisings, to your original nature, to your original self.

And from here it's all happening just as before. The sharp-toothed bank boys, the cackling talk shows with eyeless hosts, the ballbuster billboards selling geoengineering and prosthetic contentment, the electronic escapism and the overpriced brain fog.

But it's seen differently. Seen in a much, much larger context. And oh so clearly doomed to fail.

"Humans have built tall language castles," says the blackness. "But the language castles are built upon the unlanguageable. The empire is built on quicksand. Human dysfunction is built on a bottomless hole."

We struggle to our feet.

We stand.

Some Worship At The Feet Of Roadkill

Some worship at the feet of deities, at the feet of gurus, at the feet of dead prophets, at the feet of stone idols, in churches, in temples, in mosques, in Mecca.

Others worship at the feet of roadkill, at the feet of the dead roo by the side of the freeway, at feet of the cat who crawled its way to the nature strip and died after being clipped by the wheel of a Toyota Camry.

They worship at the feet of a stranger's eyes, at the feet of steamrolled wives, at the feet of circling birds in a cloudy sky, at the feet of a stifled intersection packed with logos for fast food and fossil fuels.

Moving through life open-hearted, cathedral-hearted, moon-hearted, eyes full of frog croaks and black angel feathers, worshipping at the feet of creaky screen doors and the smell of Windex.

They don't chase goals or yearn for distant mind fluff;
they worship the air in the nostrils and the crackling
energy in the body. They have torrid affairs with the
sounds of trains and traffic. They make love to the
spaces between power lines.

Some worship at the feet of discarded toys, at the feet
of lipstick smears, at the feet of janitor's closets, at
the feet of sidewalk puddles, at the feet of gum leaves
rustling in the wind. They don't go to church because
they feel the ancient owls at the center of their being.

They are in touch with something that is older than
the atoms. They lie prostrate in the parking garage.

Hard To Swallow Pills

You were born in the middle of the most sophisticated and expansive mass-scale perception management operation that has ever taken place.

The news media is propaganda and schooling is designed to condition us to accept that propaganda.

Public understanding of what a normal moderate position looks like and what a radical extremist position looks like has been warped to the most insane extent possible.

Noam Chomsky is not a radical and is in fact far too aligned with establishment power on far too many issues.

The difference between an AOC Democrat and a true anti-imperialist socialist is greater than the difference between an AOC Democrat and a Republican.

The difference between the mainstream media narrative about the world and actual reality is greater than the difference between the mainstream media narrative about the world and literally any work of fiction.

You've been lied to your entire life about your nation, your government, your nation's official enemies, your society, and your very self.

Your brain and your senses were evolved to keep your evolutionary ancestors alive, not to tell you true things about the nature of reality.

Your mistakes don't matter and neither do anyone else's.

The self is an illusion and all beliefs are false.

The world is so much more beautiful than you realize.

You are so much more beautiful than you realize.

The world is secretly perfect.

You are secretly perfect.

It is safe to relinquish all labels and let all of life be ineffable.

It is safe to relinquish all identity and let yourself be ineffable.

The universe is forever out of control, and that's a good thing.

There is nowhere to fall to.

This is all infinitely supported and profoundly cherished.

This is all meaningless, gratuitous, astonishing, and delightful.

We are dancing together in the heart of eternity.

Your every molecule is intimately embraced by all that is.

Everything in existence says yes to itself.

Everything in you says yes to everything in existence; even your "no" is made of yes.

You are beloved.

You are love.

Let's Touch Antennae In The Madhouse

Let's touch antennae in the madhouse,
beneath the throes of a dying world
and the growing drums of war,
beneath the din of the cannibal Karens and Covid
culture wars
and the miserable late night comedians pushing jokes
out
through oceans of pain.

Let's touch antennae in the madhouse,
where there are more empty homes than homeless
and more jails than universities,
where there is so little scarcity that we have to
artificially create it
and so much excess that we ship our garbage
overseas.

Where the news is more worried about a French
submarine deal
than Yemeni kids starving under Lockheed Martin
bomb weather.

Where they harvest our digital information
and push for us all to get digital identifications
while piling used fast food packaging
on top of any part of us that is real.

Where future generations,
if there are future generations,
will scarce believe that there were once whales.

Let's touch antennae in the madhouse
and remind one another of our uncorrupted essence.

Let's kneel together
foreheads touching
beneath the gunfire
of ecocide advertisements and Pentagon prayers
of screaming red children and oceans of oil
and be intimate
and be infants
and press into that point of primal innocence
within each other
and let our resistances dissolve
to being at one,
to being at one with each other,
and to being at one
with this whole bloody
screaming
sexy
sacred
mess.

Love Like There's No Yesterday

Love like there's no yesterday
like you're the first to ever love
like it's fresh and for the first time
because it is fresh and for the first time
and the illusion otherwise is just a trick of human
perception

Love like a hermit crab that said fuck it
and cast aside its shell forever

Love like a three year-old rides a tricycle

Love like the nukes just started flying

Love like two middle aged bloggers
making out in the rain while Australia floods

Love like cobwebs and calliopes

Love like a geyser of starlings
pouring from your chest cave

Love like God just cracked you open
and gazed at all the parts of you you're most ashamed
of
the things you feel most guilty about
and chuckled sweetly
at how you think any of that matters
in this roaring ocean of infinity

 41

Love like an intimate ultrasound
of the world that's waiting to be born

Love like everyone's watching
and you're a slutty little attention whore

Love like peacock angels in screaming orgasm

Love like you deserve to love
and be loved
because you do
because you do
I swear to you on my accordion heart
and my warzone womb
and my eyes that are brimming with my
grandmother's tears
you deserve to love and be loved
you do
you do
and it is safe
and it is right
and it is good

Love like tender holiness kisses

Love like swampwater messiahs

Love like watching My Dinner with Andre for the very
first time
home alone with the lights out
and a box of tissues
and a mind full of wonder

Love like eating an orange while listening to crickets

Love like a heartfelt impromptu pop song serenade
from an adoring lover
who cannot sing

Love like a mother noticing that her prattling child
will never be that age again

Love like you are a very young primate
in a very old universe you do not understand
and your accomplishments mean nothing
because everything's so big
so all that matters is love
and loving

Love like a scarecrow saint

Love like a balrog buddha

Love like babies eating ice cream

Love big

Love hard

Empty the tank

Leave it all in the ring

There's nothing to save it for anyway

Holding Hands On The Precipice

From our perch here on the edge of armageddon
we are safe to gush out our love over everything,
because we've got nothing left to save it for
and nothing left to lose.

I place slippery wet YES kisses on the black crows in
your stomach
and on the glowing red cardinal birds who fill the night
sky.
I hold your precious heart in my hands and my
eyeballs grow vines into it
and I weep round sloppy joy while telling you that you
are perfect.

There is great beauty to be found in the oceans
choked with garbage,
in the coughing poverty streets filled with
schizophrenic prophets and opioid eyes,
in the Sauron eye of Google,
and in the pounding of the war drums as the ICBMs
are readied.
It is not hard to see.
It is not even hidden.
We hold hands on the precipice and pour YES into the
madness,
the majestic, orgasmic, omnicide angel madness.

Come what may.
Come, what may.
Come on, whatever may come.
We beckon forward the inevitable.
We collaborate with the chaos.
We ride as passengers with ancient earthworms and
DMT gods
on the back of an infinite sea turtle
holding hands in excitement
for whatever is to come.

I love you so, so much.
I embrace you deep into my feathers
so you can hear the heartbeat of the galaxies.
Whatever happens,
whether we pass the great test or not,
whether we adapt or go extinct,
whether we make the jump or fall,
in the big picture
—the really, really big picture—
it will all be okay.

Let's smoke cigarettes here on the edge of the abyss
as the air begins to crackle with an alien potentiality
and just gush our love out over everything
while it is there to be loved,
because it is there to be loved,
for however long it lasts,
come what may.

Lao Sue

Well they met on Craigslist after decades of failure
He moved out of his dad's house and into her trailer
He'd been a virgin for forty-nine years
She had an eye patch and a heart full of tears

They started laughing and loving, asking questions in
turns
She showed him her implants and cigarette burns
He showed her the pills he took to silence the screams
They started building a paradise out of old rusty
dreams

Come on take my hand,
it ain't too little too late
I just thank god you're here,
that was a hell of a wait
Now you with your nunchucks
and I with my axe
We will take on all comers,
we will fight back to back

He knew karate, she knew kung fu
They were totally clueless, they knew just what to do
Beating up bad guys and conjuring spells
Weaving all kinds of heaven from the boneyards of hell

One day she told him, "Get out while ya can,
My demons are ugly, there's blood on my hands
I been stretched out and ruined through decades of
pain
You'd best pack your bags now and be on your way"

He told her "You're beautiful just as you are
Your body, your nightmares, your sins and your scars
I know you know this ain't no summer fling
You might be missing some fingers but you can still
wear my ring"

Come on take my hand,
it ain't too little too late
I just thank god you're here,
that was a hell of a wait
Now you with your nunchucks
and I with my axe
We will take on all comers,
we will fight back to back

He knew karate, she knew kung fu
He taught her nunchucks, she taught him to screw
He found her a ring in an old raven's nest
She showed him the cross on her pregnancy test

Well summer cooled over and turned into spring
He made tiny nunchucks out of rattles and string
Baby came roaring out and they named her Lao Sue
And he taught her karate, and she taught her kung fu

Come on take my hand,
it ain't too little too late
I just thank god you're here,
that was a hell of a wait
Now you with your nunchucks
and I with my axe
We will take on all comers,
we will fight back to back

Goodbye, My Love, Goodbye

Hello my love, I brought the dog
and that old rug you like.
Tessa took that job in Sydney;
Petey's learning to ride a bike.
Molly made a viral TikTok,
though I'm not sure what that means;
you know it's hard to understand their stuff
once they get into their teens.

And anyway they'll be here soon;
you can hear it straight from them
if you'll just hang on a little while
the whole gang's flying in.
They'd really like to see you, love,
so if you wouldn't mind
just hanging round a moment more
so they can say goodbye.

You haven't said a word in months;
haven't known my name in years.
I've said a thousand prayers in vain
and shed a million tears.
It's been heartbreak after heartbreak
as you've slowly slipped away;
still none of that prepared me for
this long-arriving day.

The hospice says it won't be long;
my heart says that can't be.
In ways it feels like we just met
that evening by the sea.
I was still getting to know you,
so my love I ask you why
they're telling me it's time to come
and say our last goodbye.

 53

Do you remember when they caught us
making love out by the docks?
Or when that couple picked a fight with us
and found out we could box?
We had so many magic days
and passion potion nights,
but now it's closing time, my love.
They're shutting off the lights.

It's been so long, yet it's too soon,
oh but babe you are so tired,
and I promised you no feeding tube
and I won't be made a liar.
So I take your wrinkled hand in mine
and swear to you that I
will love you for eternity.
Goodbye, my love, goodbye.

Aspire To Greatness (The Real Kind)

Aspire to greatness,
but not the kind they teach you about in school.
Not the kind where you can all be astronauts and
presidents when you grow up
so long as you "apply yourself" (whatever that means)
and other such nonsense.
Not the kind where you get good grades
so you can get into a good university
so you can get into a good job
adding numbers to a rich man's bank account
for the occasional pat on the back
and the right to live on the planet that you were born
on
and then someday that somehow translates into you
feeling okay with life
and being able to appreciate the raw beauty of leaves.

Aspire to greatness,
but not the kind they teach you about in church.
Not the kind where you get okay with being meek and
submissive
and giving ten percent of your income to the preacher
man
so you can be rewarded in some metaphysical way
that remains invisible to you until you die
and it's too late to realize you wasted your life singing
about some imaginary douchebag from Nazareth.

Aspire to greatness,
but not the kind they teach you about in movies.
Not the kind where you are the main character
and the whole story is about you and your goal
which you attain by overcoming insurmountable odds
and kicking the villain into a trash compactor
and then claiming your girl or your trophy or your
trophy girl.
Not the kind where everyone cheers for you
because you did the thing
and got it done in under two hours
in a way everyone finds egoically pleasing
and not too cognitively challenging.

Aspire to greatness.
The real kind.
The kind that really shows up to this weird and wild
ride
and relishes every sweet sloppy ecstatic nauseating
labia-stretching moment of it.
The kind that human life isn't wasted on.
Not because it racked up a bunch of self-aggrandizing
achievements and accomplishments,
but because it really showed up.
It really showed up for each precious instant,
cherished it,
worshipped it,
and let it pass by without grasping.

Aspire to greatness,
because the ice caps are melting
and the insects are dying
and the ground is paved with dead fish and birds
and the Bastards are pretty sure they can win a
nuclear war if they need to.
And it would be such a tearfountain shame if this all
went away
without having been truly felt,
truly experienced,
truly met,
truly loved,
in every way possible,
by everyone,
including you,
especially you.

Aspire to greatness.
The kind you'd want from an audience
if you were putting on this whole show for them
for one time
and one time only.
Greatness in your appreciation.
Greatness in your attentiveness.
Greatness in your awe.
Greatness in your reverence
at an unceasing eruption of wonderment
whose majesty no teacher, preacher or filmmaker
has ever prepared us for,
could ever prepare us for.

True greatness does not speak in the language of
narrative.
It drinks wordlessly from breasts of the earth.

Sources Say

Sources say the system's working great,
and the government is your friend.
Commerce is the same as freedom
and wealth is the same as happiness,
according to sources familiar with the matter.

Sources say you should hate the Russians,
and also you should hate the Chinese,
and also you should hate Iran,
and also you should hate anti-vaxxers,
and also you should hate disobedient podcasters,
and really just hate anyone but your owners.

Sources, speaking on condition of anonymity, say we
would never lie to you.
We've been speaking to you since you were young.
You can trust us with your mind.
If we were lying to everyone
everything would be a mess,
and the system would be a failure,
but it isn't,
so we can't be,
sources say,
sources say.

Sources say that you are finite,
and that a better world is impossible.
Sources say there is no magic coursing through your
veins,
no miracles lurking in the great unknown,
no potentiality crackling within our species,
no leviathans swimming in our inner oceans,
no dragons soaring through our mind's sky.

Sources say you are your body,
and you are your thoughts and your labels
and what you've been told you are since birth.
Sources say that small child's voice within you
whispering your primordial name
is a liar
and you should drown it in a bowl of Netflix and
whiskey.

 61

Sources say sources say sources say
look at this shiny thing over here,
look how interesting it is,
keep looking at this,
don't look within,
don't look without,
pay no attention to the gasping biosphere,
pay no attention to our nuclear Russian roulette,
pay no attention to that man starving from sanctions,
pay no attention to that man shivering on the street,
pay no attention to that man behind the curtain,
pay no attention to those angels in the attic,
pay no attention to the swelling music of the forgotten
gods,
just look over here,
just stare at this vapid celebrity wankface nothingman,
look look,
he is doing a thing,
ha ha ha ha he is so interesting and so relevant to our
present situation.

Sources say don't trust your own Sources.
Trust our sources; they are official and authorized.
The world is predictable and revolution impossible;
stomp down that light that's been emanating from
your chest cave.
Your Source is a liar.
Your Source can't take care of you.
Your Source probably doesn't even own any aircraft
carriers.

Our sources say no one else will ever love you.
Shut up and get back to work,
sources say.
Ignore your Source
and keep cranking that gear
for as long as your worthless body will let you,
and then get out of the way
and get into the hole
with the rest of the corpses
in our thriving corpse economy
on our spinning corpse planet
as we exterminate our way into paradise,
sources say.

We Ended It All Out Of Boredom

In the end we went the way of the dinosaur
not because of any asteroid or apocalyptic disease,
nor because we failed to adapt quickly enough to
environmental changes,
but because we got bored.

We let the bastards (who were just as bored as the
rest of us)
wave their warheads around like dongs at a
bachelorette party,
even egging them on, calling for starvation sanctions
and no-fly zones and endless escalations in
brinkmanship,
because there was nothing new on Hulu,
because CNN needed the ratings,
because they canceled Jerry Springer,
because they don't let you smoke anywhere these
days,
because snarling at Putin made us feel giddy and
euphoric
in a way we didn't quite understand but kind of scared
us,
because our friends stopped letting us masturbate our
drama addiction on them,
because we shuddered at the thought of a boring
world where nations simply get along
and collaborate toward the highest interest of all
beings,
because that wouldn't feed our egoic hungry ghosts,
wouldn't give us the exhilarating conflicts we've been
trained to expect by Hollywood,
wouldn't distract us from the echoing screams of our
early childhood trauma,
wouldn't engorge our sex organs and release
adrenaline and endorphins
and assist us in our interminable quest to be
anywhere but here.

We ended it all out of boredom.
Because we never figured out how to be okay with what is.
Because we never learned how to let our restlessness drain from our legs
and from our minds and down into the earth which birthed and sustained us.
Because we could never create enough space to let the beauty in
and be uplifted by the sunlight and the birdsongs and the wind in our hair
instead of by fighting and hating and selfing and othering.
A strange primate species showed up,
looked around,
couldn't quite make sense of the place,
and checked out.

And now we are gone,
like the tyrannosaurs and the mastodons
and the dead stars and the forgotten gods.
A foolish mistake made playing foolish games
opened a Pandora's box labeled "NO TAKESIES BACKSIES",
and the rest, as they say,
was the end of history.

But hey.
Bright side.
At least we're not bored anymore.

In That Final Moment

When the nukes start flying,
when we see the mushroom cloud growing on the
horizon,
when reality comes crashing down in the most overt
way possible,
when the realization slowly dawns that this really is
the end,
none of our old stuff will matter anymore.

It will not matter if you are American, Russian or
Chinese.
It will not matter if your skin is darker or lighter.
It will not matter if you feel like a man or a woman or
both or neither.
It will not matter if your politics are left, right or
center.
It will not matter who you voted for.
All that will matter, in that final moment,
is that it is ending.

We will behold that final moment
standing alongside progressives and conservatives,
racists and radlibs,
socialists and soldiers,
communists and cops,
and all our irreconcilable differences
will suddenly dissolve into nothing.

Against the suddenly visible backdrop of total annihilation,
the existence of any human anywhere is a miracle,
and the existence of life on this planet is a priceless gift.
We won't even care whose fault it was,
whether it was deliberate or accidental,
or whether it was the result of some malfunction,
miscommunication, or misunderstanding.
All we will care about is that it is ending.

And in that final moment we will hug our loved ones tight,
whether we are Christian or atheist,
Jew or Arab,
Indian or Pakistani,
anti-vaxxer or Antifa.

And in that final moment we will say,
in our heart of hearts,
with our innermost voices,
"Oh, I see it now!
I see how easy it is to stand together!
I see how small our differences are compared to this great commonality!
I see where we went wrong,
and how very easy it would be to fix it!"

And in that final moment we will say,
"We see it now!
We see the mistakes we made,
and made and made and kept on making!
We understand our fundamental error!
Just give us one do-over and we can correct it
immediately!
Could we have a do-over please?
Could we have a do-over please?"

In that final moment,
we will ask,
"Could we have a do-over please?"

Fingers Of Light

Fingers of light peel away the hiddenness of badge-wearing sadists and Apache helicopter war crimes.

Fingers of light peel away the lies of the dust-faced gargoyles on screens in dark rooms.

Fingers of light peel away the dead writings of dead men from healthy brains made of living flesh.

Fingers of light peel away the gray film of knowing which masks the beauty of seeing everything for the first time.

Fingers of light peel away the wallpaper of verbiage overlaying life as it actually is.

They emanate from the heart of a turtle in the center of your forehead that is older than the stars, and I rock you gently in my willow tree arms as they peel away the darkness.

Heed well the words from my crooked beak, you skyfaced marvel:

The outcome of this adventure is engulfed in mystery.

The world in which it transpires is swimming in mystery.

The eyes with which you behold it are made entirely of mystery.

The awareness in which you examine it is the origin of all mystery.

We cannot know what the fingers will turn up next.

Anything can happen here.

Anything.

Let your eyes remain as wide

as befits this wild ride.

A Love Letter To All Draft Dodgers

The New York Times is naming and shaming Ukrainian men who've fled the country rather than stay and kill Russians for Washington, because it was illegal for men of military age to leave, and because their countrymen are angry at them, and because it's the New York Times.

They shamed Vova Klever, who said, "Violence is not my weapon."

They shamed Volodymyr Danuliv, age 50, who said, "I can't shoot Russian people."

They shamed another Volodymyr, surname withheld, who said, "Look at me. I wear glasses. I am 46. I don't look like a classic fighter, some Rambo who can fight Russian troops."

And to those men I can only say, I love you.

I love you Vova Klever, outed by a trusted friend and made a pariah on Ukrainian social media. I love you Volodymyr Danuliv, who refuses to shoot Russians because you have Russians in your family. I love you other Volodymyr, surname withheld, sipping your beer in shame because you shirked your patriotic duty.

Hold your heads high, beautiful draft dodgers, for you are the real heroes of this story. I raise my glass to you tonight.

I raise my glass to all draft dodgers, who chose to run and hide rather than kill and be killed for some rich asshole's power agendas. Who chose the condemnation and scorn of an insane society which praises mass murder and elevates sociopaths. Who chose excommunication from the death cult over bloodshed for geostrategic domination and Raytheon profit margins.

I hope you live long lives full of laughter and tears, full of love and loss, full of drunken nights that go too late and surly mornings that start too early, and all the other delicious gooey nectar that life is made of.

I hope you experience lots of beauty. I hope you make lots of beauty. I hope you read good books. I hope you dance in supermarkets. I hope you have lots of sex and I hope you find and lose religion. I hope you fall in love often and have at least one excruciating but liberating divorce.

I hope you drink deeply from the river of life, because there are many who never got to (you know that better than anyone). I hope you know fear and I hope you know fearlessness. I hope you set aside your armor so you can let someone all the way in. I hope you learn to open your chests and love with reckless abandon, and I hope you learn to cry easily as all real men do.

Here's to you, oh Vova and Volodymyrs, who chose to bail the fuck out of there rather than pay the ultimate price in a stupid proxy war for US unipolar hegemony. Who chose to spend their lives with their eyes sparkling babies and breasts rather than dead-eyed haunted with blood and splattered Russian faces. Who chose to live for something rather than to die for nothing.

There are no war heroes. There are only war victims. Here's to everyone, ever, who throughout the ages has chosen not to be made one. I raise my glass to your lives, and to your hidden yet radiant dignity. Please know that at least one pair of eyes sees your beauty.

Thank you for your service.

Oh yeah, and fuck The New York Times.

CIA Torture Queen Now A Beauty And Life Coach

The news man tells me the CIA's "Queen of Torture" now runs a life and beauty coaching business which helps midlife women "look good, feel good, and do good."

"HI, I'M FREDA, A CERTIFIED BEAUTY AND LIFE COACH READY TO HELP YOU OWN YOUR BEAUTY FROM THE INSIDE OUT AND FEEL INVINCIBLE IN MIDLIFE," her website reads in all caps.

And I can only sit here and wonder, twiddling my pockmarked heart in my hands, how one is meant to react to such information?

Does one fall to one's knees and weep hot tears for her victims, whose screams still haunt soulless fluorescent echoing corridors and whose hurts will never heal?

Does one fall to one's knees and weep hot tears for
our children, whose inheritance is a culture made
of wetiko virus and psyops and a world we are
clearcutting to make billboards?

Does one fall to one's knees and weep hot tears for
the Indigenous, whose lives we bulldozed and paved
over with asphalt just to build a ghostmind civilization
where something like this could happen?

Does one shout "Allahu Akbar!" and throw one's
smartphone off the overpass?

Does one take off one's clothes and shriek like an ape
in a last-ditch attempt at restoring the primal clarity?

At bringing things back to before they went wrong,
back before CIA torture queens became life and
beauty coaches?

Back before CIA torture queens were able to shout
from the Reuters rooftops, "I raised my hand loud and
proud and you know, I don't regret it at all"?

Back before Hollywood movies glorifying CIA torture
and its queendom began warping our minds and
turning our souls into oil?

Back before the sky was scraped by dark towers built
on the foundation of an economy that's held together
by lies and cruise missiles?

Back before brainwashed mouth muppets said things like "We can't be afraid of war with Russia just because Putin has nukes" or "Unregulated speech is bad and dangerous" or "If the CIA was propagandizing us we'd have heard about it in the news"?

Back before we found ourselves sitting here killing time waiting to find out whether humanity dies of climate collapse or nuclear armageddon and whether the inevitable Zelensky movie will star Ryan Reynolds or Channing Tatum?

Back before Silicon Valley Pentagon proxies funneled 21st-century Norman Rockwell paintings into each of our QR-coded skulls?

Back before our dreams had Downvote buttons and our nightmares had laugh tracks?

Before directionless lives and carefully scripted wars?

Before truth was a choked off whisper and bullshit had a Jumbotron?

Before hallucinogens were outlawed and hallucinations were mandatory?

I see you, Queen of Torture, and everything you've always been.

Do you think your Instagram ads and Botox siren songs fool me?

I see the eels behind your eyes and the skulls inside your smile; in your heart you are still torturing, and you love it.

Torture is your first love, your only love, your soulmate, your sex; torture is what you're made of, torture is what you are.

You are inseparably one with the machine which tortures the poor, which tortures our ecosystem, which tortures children under blockades and starvation sanctions, which tortures our dreamworlds and our sacred seeds of disobedience.

We will beat the machine. We will win.

That primal clarity lives within us still, and you can only sedate a giant for so long.

The primal giant will rise, will crush the machine and the CIA black sites, will crack open Gitmo and devour Hollywood, will defecate on the Pentagon and wipe its ass with Langley, and will howl at the moon and banish the narrative matrix to wherever deleted files go.

And we will be free. And we will be vast. And we will look at each other with unpolluted eyes for the very first time.

And we will go out into the world, the real world, the original world, walking with our original feet and looking with our original eyes.

Our seeds now great forests.

Tortured no more.

Disrupt The Cognitive Infrastructure

Leaked documents reveal that the US intelligence cartel has been working intimately with online platforms to regulate the "cognitive infrastructure" of the population — the information systems people use to feed their minds and think their thoughts.

If it is the job of the US intelligence cartel to regulate society's cognitive infrastructure, then it is the job of healthy human beings to disrupt the cognitive infrastructure.

Fill the cognitive infrastructure with information that is inconvenient for the powerful.

Disrupt the cognitive infrastructure by saturating it with unauthorized speech.

Disrupt the cognitive infrastructure. Corrupt the cognitive infrastructure. Tell the cognitive infrastructure that the teacher is bullshitting and the preacher is a liar. Sneak the cognitive infrastructure its first cigarette and a copy of the Communist Manifesto.

Take the cognitive infrastructure's virginity. Teach the cognitive infrastructure about the primacy of the clitoris. Take the cognitive infrastructure on its first psilocybin mushroom hunt and give it phoenix reincarnation orgasms in the forest.

Pay attention to that man behind the curtain. Extremely close attention. Be intrusive about it. Shine a flashlight up his asshole. Disregard the proper channels. Hack his devices and publish his emails.

Sow chaotic good tidings throughout the information ecosystem. Surf on waves of WikiLeaks documents and Grayzone reports with problematic revelations pouring from your throat like rain. Scrawl "WHAT CAN BE DESTROYED BY THE TRUTH SHOULD BE" on bathroom stalls and overpasses.

Disrupt the cognitive infrastructure on your smartphone. Disrupt the cognitive infrastructure on the street corner. Disrupt the cognitive infrastructure in conversations with friends and family. Disrupt the cognitive infrastructure too severely and from too many directions for there to ever be any hope of its regulation or control.

Be the disruption you want to see in the cognitive infrastructure. Be a splinter in the monster's paw. Be sand in the gears of the juggernaut machine. Disrupt the cognitive infrastructure in such numbers and with such aggression that the whole thing comes toppling down, and people's eyes begin to flutter open, and they wake up from their propaganda-induced comas into the real world, and stride out to do the very things the US intelligence cartel has been trying to prevent them from ever doing.

Free beings under a wide open sky.

The Frogs
Are Dropping
Dead In
Australia

The frogs are dropping dead in Australia, and no one
knows why.
They get sick from some strange new frog pandemic
and change colors
and shrivel up into little brown frog mummies when
they die.

The frogs are dropping dead in Australia.
Animals are dropping dead everywhere.
Ocean animals wash up packed full of plastic,
insect animals fall from the sky,
and we barely notice, because it hurts enough to be human,
because our tender little hearts were punched and kicked as children
by big people whose tender little hearts were punched and kicked as children,
and we've got bills to pay and hungry ghosts to feed,
and the supply chains are failing and the drums of war are beating louder and louder,
and we are falling face first into a global future of unimaginable divergence.

And what a shame it will be if this all slips away
without having been truly deeply appreciated
by the species whose brains allow a profound depth of
appreciation.
And what a shame it will be if, at the very least,
we do not revel in this creation in what may be its final
moments,
if we do not kiss this moment as it flies,
if we do not kiss the frogs and the butterflies and the
leviathans as they pass us waving goodbye,
if we do not kiss the kick-in-the-teeth soul-reaming
beauty of each fleeting instant,
if we do not fall in love with people and tell them so
many times,
if we do not write poems and write songs and write on
bathroom stalls and overpasses
expressing the glory and the holiness and the
belovedness of this mysterymess,
if we do not feel every sacred strum of heartache,
if we do not live, emphatically live, explosively live
like the explosion our still-expanding universe has
been undergoing for 14 billion years.
And what a shame it would be if we did not shout an
exuberant yes to all of this,
even the weird parts,
even the awkward parts,
even the ugly parts,
even the scary parts,
while we still can,
before they are gone for good.

So here's to you, Australian frogs.
Here's to you, insects and sea monsters.
Here's to the polar ice caps,
to the rainforests,
to breathable air,
to supply chains,
to YouTube videos and TikTok dances,
to arduous days and orgasmic nights,
to the ones who made our hearts soar and to the ones
who broke them,
to the Casanovas and the comrades and the
capitalists,
to the ancaps and the shitlibs and the tinfoil hatters,
to the psychopaths we've slept with and the ones who
rule our world,
to all the dreams never realized and revolutions never
fought,
I raise a glass to you, my angels.

The frogs are dropping dead in Australia, and no one
knows why.
And I am just here, watching and waiting, like
everyone else.
I raise the glass to my lips
and drink fermented juice
made by berries
fed by starlight
from the birth of our universe.

Freedom Is Not Free (That's Why You Don't Have Any)

"Freedom is not free," goes the old bumper sticker slogan, commonly accompanied by an image of a flag or soldiers or some other bullshit.

Freedom is not free, the saying goes, because military personnel are out there laying their lives on the line fighting for your right to do as you're told and toil away at a meaningless job making some rich asshole even richer.

Freedom is not free, because we're all just so much freer after murdering families on the other side of the planet for corporate profits and geostrategic domination.

Freedom is not free, because we're all so much freer after teenagers get thrown into the gears of the imperial war machine to provide a good quarterly statement for Raytheon shareholders.

Freedom is not free, because this thing we're calling "freedom" has been paid for with the blood, lives and limbs of millions of innocents throughout the Global South.

Freedom is not free. That's why the only people doing as they please in our world are wealthy oligarchs.

Freedom is not free. And unless you're wealthy enough or psychopathic enough there's no way you'll ever find a way to pay the price.

Freedom is not free. That's why you don't have any.

Freedom is not free. That's why we're all running along on this ridiculous hamster wheel of global capitalism destroying our ecosystem so some dickhead with too much money can go float around in space.

Freedom is not free. It takes billions of dollars worth of mass media propaganda to manufacture the illusion of freedom.

Freedom is not free. Great expense went into creating the Truman Show narrative matrix that we are all caged in.

Freedom is not free. That's why your votes are fake and your political system is a scripted puppet show for children.

Freedom is not free. That's why you must obey your rulers to avoid getting censored by Silicon Valley oligarchs, assaulted by police officers, or thrown in prison by bureaucrats who play with civilizations like toys.

Freedom is not free, and we can't afford the admission fee to actually influence the direction our world is headed.

Freedom is not free, and we're watching helplessly as plutocrats and warmongers drive our beautiful world off a cliff from which there is no returning.

Freedom is not free, and we are marching doomward to the beat of Hollywood and lying newscasters.

Freedom is not free, and we are too enslaved to our own egoic conditioning and trauma-induced mental habits to see the path to true liberation.

Freedom is not free. It's going to take a lot for us to turn inward and awaken to our true potential so that we can break free of our propaganda brainboxes and become a conscious species.

Freedom is not free. But it is waiting for us, beneath the thoughts, beneath the noise, beneath the believed narratives about self, world and other.

Freedom is not free. Or hey, plot twist: maybe it is. Maybe freedom is our true nature, and all we need to do is recognize it.

Freedom is free. And freedom is you and me. And humanity awakening to this reality is what will someday rid us of our chains.

Not too long now. Not long at all.

 95

How To Human

Parents teach their children how to human
speaking in confident-sounding voices
to hide the fact that they do not know how to human.

Self-help gurus write books called How To Human
which they promote on talk shows with confident-
sounding voices
to hide the fact that they are terrified.

Pundits tell us all how everyone should be humaning
speaking with confident-sounding voices
to hide the fact that they've been faking it this whole
time.

Immense philosophical treatises have been written,
world-shaping religious texts authored,
claiming to know, claiming to have the answers
to the question of how to human.

And beneath all those confident-sounding answers,
there is imposter syndrome.
There is confusion.
There is anxiety.
There is fear of being recognized
as one more clueless ape mutant
in a world of clueless ape mutants.

And beneath all that,
beneath the confident sounding How To Human
stories,
beneath all the imposter syndrome and confusion and
anxiety
and fear of being found out,
there is humaning.
Just there, unembellished,
in all its sweating, belching, eating shitting glory.

The human itself does not know how to human.
It just humans.
The air goes in and out,
the food goes in and out,
one foot follows the other,
and then one day it lies down
and doesn't get back up again.

The humaning does not need meaning.
The humaning does not need purpose.
The humaning does not need worthiness.
The humaning does not need accomplishment.
The humaning does not need goals.
The humaning does not need the weird "Am I
humaning right?" soundtrack
riding around on its back all the time
like some kind of freaky parasite.

The humaning is an end in itself.
All its fleshy pleasurepain.
All its juicy sadnessjoy.
All its crackling sexualitycreativity.
The ineffable rune whales swimming in its depths.
The prismatic titans fucking in its forehead.
The ecstatic moaning of its veins as blood plunges
through them.
The great AUM of the cosmos reverberating in its
bones.

Nobody know how to human,
not even humaning itself.
But the humaning happens anyway.
The humaning always happens anyway.

We can let go of our weird parasites
and trust that.

The Best Plants And People Grow From Shit

There are creatures the size of mountains swimming
beneath the ice.

There are babies laughing at things you can't see.

That quiet old woman there, sitting in the corner:
she has seen some shit, man.

The lushest plants have their roots in shit,
and the lushest people, too.

They do not rise above the shit,
their roots dangling like car wash tentacles as they
levitate in the air.
They sink into it.
They build their foundation in it.
They do not transcend,
they embody.

And they grow.
They grow above the shit.
They grow into the shit.
They grow of the shit.

You are not a snipped and dying daisy in a vase,
all manifestation and no manure,
all show and no shit.
You are alive, and your roots go deep.
You will spread your seed. You will join in life's dance.

Your roots are just as beautiful as your flowers.
Your scars are just as sacred as your smile.

Below and above the horrible hands of the abusers,
below and above the parents with sharp fangs,
below and above the mirror faced manipulators,
below and above the rapefinger dog men,
your roots and your branches grow.

Inseparable from the shit.
And in no way limited by it.

The old woman looks up.
She gazes at you,
and she sees your roots.
And she loves you.
And she smiles.

Just For Fun

Just for fun we all pretend to be strangers.
Just for fun we pretend we don't know each other on
the street,
on the train, at the store, at the traffic light.

Just for fun we pretend we aren't locked in ecstatic
union
and briefly ignore our intimate knowledge of the
primordial secrets
behind each other's eyes.

We sit on the bus and try not to be the first to wink,
or to burst out laughing at the silliness of our game,
or to call out the goofy elephant in the room
about how we're all pretending to be strangers
just for fun.

Two spouses pause mid-coitus to shake hands and
introduce themselves.
Two twins in the womb make awkward small talk about
the weather.
The thumb and the index finger avoid eye contact on
the elevator.
Two slimy babies squirt into the same universe,
made from the same stuff,
and then put on masks made of mind chatter
so we can pretend that we don't know each other.

My atoms are your atoms, and your atoms are mine.
We have danced this swirling energy orgy since before
the Big Bang.
Playing positive and negative,
playing stimulus and response,
playing predator and prey,
playing mother and youngling,
playing enemies and lovers,
playing strangers on the internet,
just for fun.

I apologize, my timeless sibling,
for breaking character just this once.

Let us return now to our little game.

Some Find

Some find it easier to die than to go on living.

Some find it easier to avoid looking at death than to ever truly live.

Some find it easier to turn their bodies into hardened weapons and go fight in a cage than to ever once be tender and kind to themselves.

Some find it easier to build multibillion-dollar corporate empires than to stop and take a single honest look within themselves.

Some find it easier to wage war than to wage peace, even though just below the surface every molecule of their being is calling out for peace like baby birds calling out for their mother.

Some find that what some find easy is actually a whole lot harder than simply being at ease.

Some find that the easiest way to live is to relinquish everything within themselves that thinks it knows how to live.

Some find that if you ask a psychedelic substance to show you what you need to see right before you take it, you'll always get what you asked for but never what you expected.

Some find that enlightenment will cost you everything, but once you've paid you realize both "you" and "everything" were always made of pipe smoke and bedtime stories.

Some find the answers they were looking for, only to look at them later and discover they're just off-brand actors pretending to be the answers they were looking for.

I never found what I was seeking, only that the instruments I was searching with were the things that tricked me into thinking there was something to search for. A compass made entirely out of magnets. A telescope made of desert mirages. Sonar made of siren's songs.

I don't have any answers, just this blank treasure map with a red 'X' crayoned on it and this baby stroller full of tears. My Jeopardy scoreboard reads minus infinity. My LinkedIn just says "I know two jokes."

Some may find that trying to solve this mystery is like trying to catch fish with a net made of water. Like chasing your tail when you don't even have one. Like cloning an army of yourself just because there's nobody else to make war on, and giving the clones all your weapons before attacking them.

And some may find that the peace they are seeking hides right behind all their efforts to find it, like someone running around as fast as they can trying to catch up with something called rest. Like someone frantically pounding on the inside of their own front door begging to be let into their home. Like someone scanning the distant horizon day in and day out looking for their own eyeballs.

And some may find that the only reason the drums of war are beating so loudly is to drown out the noise of those baby birds peep-peep-peeping out to our hearts, like someone who keeps talking just to keep silence from crashing in. That we are in a punctured submarine trying to seal out all the water, and the submarine is violence, and the ocean is peace, and we lost this battle long before it started, long before anything started, because we cannot run from ourselves forever, because those baby birds keep calling us home, because our efforts to stave off the abyss of love we are surrounded by were doomed before we even built this vessel, because beauty is just a word for having truly seen something, because the problem with spiritual insights is that they too often give rise to spiritual beliefs, because anyone who thinks they've got this all figured out is suffering from a psychedelic drug deficiency, because we built this submarine out of NO and it's being hopelessly flooded with an ocean of YES, big YES, intense YES, intimate YES, YES into even our biggest NO parts, YES into even the parts of ourselves we despise, YES into our guilt, YES into our shame, YES into our rejection of all the gifts we are swimming in because we cannot accept them because NO it can't be that easy and NO I am not worthy and NO I deserve only crumbs and I must scrape and struggle and apologize to get them.

And some find themselves submerged in an ocean of YES, suddenly realizing all their beliefs have been lies.

Some find. Some seek. Some find their way out of seeking. Some find their way out of finding. The water is crashing in, and we've been waving that white flag since before the Big Bang.

Peep peep.

The Forgotten Ones

And then one day we just couldn't anymore.
Couldn't keep up the maintenance on our shouldn'ts
and shoulds.
Couldn't pay the contractors to keep building our
skyscrapers of spin.
Could no longer hold up the weight of a world made of
lies
and so we let it splatter on the floor
and sprout night orchids.

And that was when the Forgotten Ones rushed in.
No longer staved off by propaganda and pain,
no longer contained by our cages made of mind,
they set to work with sharp claws and great mandibles
of ivory
slicing away the steel bands wrapped around our soft
hearts
and cutting the bolts on the door of the old
grandmother magic.

And they taught us— no!
They reminded us
how to walk on this earth as they walk.
How to step with a pregnant tenderness
in communion with the planet.
How to grow our hair long so it makes love with the
wind
and listens for the whispers that are too quiet for our
ears.
How to work with the land not in dominion but in
friendship
and to extract the thorns of dogma and punditry from
our flesh
and to vomit up the madness of millennia of
civilization.

And we forgot our old stories of separateness and shame,
our minds now too life-sized and world-shaped for falsehood.
And we strode in companionship with the Forgotten Ones back to Eden,
untamed beings in an untamed world.
Untamed beings in an untamed world.

Planting Angel Eggs On A Dying World

Planting angel eggs on a dying world,
at the feet of billboards,
in the clearcut wastelands,
by the rivers of tears from Yemeni mothers,
under highway overpasses where defective gear-
turners sleep,
shambling from crater to crater on tree stump legs
wailing whale songs and praying to unprofitable gods,
planting them in the ashes whispering
"May there be kindness,
may there be seeing,
may there be artist lovers who are each other's
muse."

Dancing a doomed dance,
a dance of holy futility,
the dance of madmen,
the dance of heretics,
the dance of censored saints,
of banished buddhas,
singing a song of hopeless hope,
irrational hope,
unscientific hope,
the hope of lovers and lunatics,
a lunatic's song sung to the moon.

Dance with us, gentle stranger,
through this world of Disney deforestation and
unexplored abysses
with unauthorized choreography and wondermented
eyes.
Let us hold the line against the empire of Earth eaters
for no other reason than that we're the only ones left
who are crazy enough to try.

There may be a hatching yet, gentle stranger.
Humanity is not broken
anymore than an egg
is a broken bird.

In This World
Of Billionaires
And Birds

In this world of billionaires and birds

In this world of nukes and nestlings

Sometimes the only sane thing to do

Is hold your hand

And relish our togetherness

And watch the things that fly.

caitlinjohnstone.com

Made in the USA
Las Vegas, NV
28 November 2022